THE LUCKIEST GUY IN THE WORLD

THE LUCKIEST GUY IN THE WORLD

RAYMOND D. LOEWE

iUniverse, Inc.
Bloomington

The Luckiest Guy in the World

iUniverse books may be ordered through booksellers or by contacting:

iUniverse
1663 Liberty Drive
Bloomington, IN 47403
www.iuniverse.com
1-800-Authors (1-800-288-4677)

ISBN: 978-1-4759-6476-9 (sc)
ISBN: 978-1-4759-6477-6 (ebk)

Library of Congress Control Number: 2012922661

Printed in the United States of America

iUniverse rev. date: 01/17/2013

TABLE OF CONTENTS

To my office staff, my family,
my friends, my swim coach,
my coach at Strategic
Coach®, my advisory board,
and my clients

Thank you all for
helping me
become the
luckiest guy in
the world.

CHAPTER 1

My Paradigm Shift

I *am* the luckiest guy in the world! I travel several times a year to fascinating places, I have developed (no pun intended) a hobby in photography and won prizes for my photos. I am in good health, and I'm an All-American Masters Swimmer. I have a financial planning practice with clients I enjoy and at this point in my life (age seventy) I, not only, have no plans to retire, but my business is in growth mode.

How did I get to this place? I owe much of it to an entrepreneurial coaching program I joined about fifteen years ago. In this program I had to unlearn many of the traditional practices of the financial-services industry, as well as many accepted ideas in our society. It was a 180-degree turn, but well worth the effort.

One of the hardest changes was how I manage my time. I learned that I needed to take more time off to recharge and rejuvenate myself. I also learned the importance of finding more time for the things I wanted to do by delegating things I wasn't very good at doing to people who were. And I accepted that I needed to refine my client list so I could streamline my practice to be more efficient.

All of this didn't happen overnight. In fact the transition took more time than I expected. But once I recognized the benefits the changes brought, each new change was a little easier.

Because I gained more free time, I needed to find ways to spend it. My wife, Sandy, and I booked several trips, but we quickly discovered that trips without a purpose didn't work too well for us. So when a client, who is a college professor devoted to protecting and saving the nesting beaches of the leatherback turtles, invited us to visit his beach/lab in Costa Rica, we thought it would be interesting. We were right! We were so right that we immediately began planning to find more travel destinations that would include an educational component.

Within a year or two of embarking on our travels, I decided to polish my skills with a camera. It began slowly, but a hobby was born. We traveled to the Arctic to photograph polar bears and, on another occasion, the Aurora Borealis. We climbed down into slot canyons in Utah to photograph rock formations with brilliant coloring and came home with amazing photos. Travel to China gave us the opportunity to spend time with local farmers and to experience the awe of seeing the Terracotta Warriors.

We photographed the magnificence of the Balloon Fiesta in Albuquerque and went to the Baja Peninsula, in California, Mexico, to photograph whales. We actually got to pet the playful calves that the mother whales seemed to push toward the Zodiac rafts. It was amazing. And our most recent journey found us in Africa on the photographic trail of lions, elephants, giraffes, and leopards.

What's ahead? Ireland is booked as well as a unique photo tour of Yellowstone National Park. My wish list for the future includes a trip to Antarctica to photograph Emperor penguins. And just recently an acquaintance I met at a swim competition piqued my interest in visiting

Nepal. If I book a trip to Australia, I will have set foot on each of the seven continents.

A very exciting development from my trip to Africa is a project I'm working on with a field researcher I met there. As part of his doctoral work, Andrei is tracking lions and leopards using trail cameras and satellite collars. I sent him two cameras to replace those damaged by wildlife, and shortly thereafter, he sent me amazing photos from those cameras.

This got me thinking, and now my wife and I are both working on a program to create a curriculum for schools designed to motivate students to be excited about learning about the big cats in Africa. A client is designing the curriculum and will be spearheading the program.

We're also working on the early stages of a curriculum based on students interviewing centenarians to learn about history, social studies, and all the wisdom older seniors have gained.

These projects, and the value I see in bringing them to others, add excitement to my life, and I don't ever want to lose that. I hope that along with my photography hobby, my love of travel, and my lifelong commitment to competitive swimming I will continue working with my clients, meeting new clients, and helping all of them redefine their lives so they are as excited about things as I am. I will never jump off the retirement cliff!

CHAPTER 2

Money is a Tool

I've been so blessed with the way my life has evolved that I wanted to share this opportunity with clients. My staff and I have expanded our financial-planning practice to include life planning. This has made our planning more focused and more valuable to our clients. The reason for having money now has specific meaning. ***It's directly linked to things they want to do rather than to amorphous pots of money.***

When we talk with our young families about this, they move up their goals. They see the value of being able to do the things they want to earlier in their lives, even if it means they have to work longer. It's gotten many of them to rethink their careers in order to accomplish this.

The sooner our clients define their "vision," the easier it is for us to design the transition. Unfortunately, many people approach retirement by working extremely hard, often in careers they simply tolerate, to accumulate money so they can stop working and have fun. I call this "cliff retirement."

Sadly, what actually happens is that they burn themselves out with no real plan for the rest of their lives. They might not have taken care of themselves health-wise, which results in boredom and declining health. Many people find that they can't do what they want to do or, worse yet, many don't even **know** what they want to do.

Instead of burning out in an unpleasant career, wouldn't it be better to make work enjoyable NOW? Wouldn't it be better to start taking time off to enjoy other facets of life NOW, even if it means extending an enjoyable work life into the future to make up for reduced revenues?

CHAPTER 3

The New Retirement Paradigm™

Before I could help my clients make this transition, I had to figure it out for myself. It took quite a few years, but when I looked back at my progress I saw the pattern.

First, I got to know myself better. This involved understanding more about my instinctive way of taking action and learning how to allow myself to do that more often and not doing things the way the educational and business worlds had taught me.

I learned to delegate more of the things I wasn't very good at, or didn't like to do, to others who were better at doing them than I was. Suddenly I had more time to strategize ways to make my business work better for me and for my clients.

With the added free time, I started looking for ways to use it. My coaching program convinced me that taking time off is critical to being a better professional and thus of greater value to my clients. True time off—no calls to the office or checking e-mail—resulted in a rejuvenation that vastly improved my brain power and my mental energy.

This led to my interest in photography and the travel I needed in order to expand my photographic opportunities.

Suffice it to say, the changes began to come more quickly and now I travel three or four times a year, I swim competitively, and I am more excited and challenged by my business than ever.

After looking back over the journey to my own New Retirement Paradigm™, I recognized the process I could implement with clients to bring them to theirs.

The New Retirement Paradigm™ is a four-step process comprised of:

1. Know yourself.
2. Redefine your work life.

3. Define your vision of your "play" life.
4. Arrange your financial infrastructure to be able to have the life you want.

By the way, I have been very gratified with my clients' responses when I share this New Retirement Paradigm™ with them. Read on for some of their stories.

Know Yourself

- Stop fighting your instincts.
- Define and work to your strengths.
- Discover your Unique Ability®*.

CHAPTER 4

Know Yourself

There are numerous facets to us that make up who we are as individuals. There are many mores that our parents, our society, and our culture have taught us.

There are also aspects of the human mind that are instinctive to us, that is to say hardwired. And instincts cannot be learned; we are born with them. We are, however, often trained to override them in favor of behaviors that our society or our culture values.

In learning who we are, it is important to recognize those true instinctive behaviors because they are inborn strengths. Working to our strengths uses less mental energy and when we do so we have more mental energy to devote to doing what is important. When we override our instinctive strengths, we get exhausted and we can suffer burnout.

I learned in my entrepreneurial coaching workshop that there are four types of things we do in our lives:

- things we're not good at and shouldn't be doing;
- things we're average at and which others do equally well or better;
- things we're excellent at doing but that take a toll on our mental energy; and
- things we're both excellent at doing and passionate about.

The things in that last category are what the founder, Dan Sullivan, of The Strategic Coach® Program calls our "Unique Ability®*". When we work in our Unique Ability®, we can literally go forever. In fact, what we are doing when we use our Unique Ability® doesn't even feel like work. Who wouldn't like to spend most of his or her time doing things he or she is excellent at and passionate about?

Often it is difficult for individuals to identify their Unique Ability®. These behaviors are so intrinsic to us that we don't even consciously know that we're doing them. We just know that some things just seem to "work."

Several tools have been developed that can help individuals zero-in on their areas of uniqueness. One tool measures how we instinctively attack a task if left to do it our own way. Another tool measures talents with which we are born. The wisdom behind both of these tools acknowledges that while we are able to disregard these instinctive behaviors and work in ways that are not natural to us, we are often less effective when doing so.

Discovering my Unique Ability® involved using these tools, and also asking family, friends, and business associates/clients what value they believed I brought to the relationships we have together. This process was quite enlightening.

I boiled all of this analysis down to: "I make people feel good about their future by sifting through the details to help them recognize what is really important." This helped me acknowledge that while I was trained to create financial plans, the task of collecting and inputting data was not a good use of my talents. However, analyzing a completed plan and integrating my understanding of the client's concerns and opportunities available allows me to communicate the plan to them in such a way that they understand and buy-in to my recommendations . . . and they feel positive about their future.

On a personal level, I realized that I was doing many things because I was capable of doing them, but that there are many others who are equally capable, if not better, at doing them. By delegating these tasks, I now have more time to spend on the things that interest me and that I'm passionate about doing.

The adage "To thine own self, be true" is so apt!

Amy's Story

I was pleased to learn that my client, Amy, had decided to practice what I was preaching. After a stint working at the White House, she completed her MBA at Harvard and landed a job with a large consulting firm. The great salary appealed to her thrifty nature and she was diligently paying off student loans and saving for her retirement. Although she enjoyed many of the facets of this job, Amy was working far more hours than she wanted to and was realizing that she had no social life.

We had been talking with Amy about the New Retirement Paradigm™ and engaged in many conversations about her finding a job that she loved and could see herself doing past traditional retirement age. We must have been getting through to her because every time we spoke with her, she surprised us with news of another trip she had just taken.

One such trip was to a dude ranch that awakened a love for the outdoors and horseback riding—activities she had enjoyed as a young girl. Amy began thinking about changing jobs and perhaps earning a little less, but also having a more normal work week, closer to forty hours. We did some planning with her and showed her that it wouldn't be the financial disaster she feared if she took a new job. And so she did take a new job.

With her newfound time, Amy began to envision her future. She now knows she would like to work for a foundation that would allow her to move to the Pacific Northwest, own a small ranch, and have a few horses. She can imagine doing this past the traditional retirement age and enjoying it.

With her new vision, Amy is now exploring how to make it a reality.

Redefine Your Work Life

- What are you good at?
- What do you like to do?
- Integrate passion and excellence.
- Create a work/play time balance.
- Where do you provide value that people really appreciate?

CHAPTER 5

Define Your Ideal Work Life

Armed with a better understanding of what makes us unique, the next step in the process is to look at our work life and make some decisions.

How we treat work can be critically important. How much we work obviously affects how much time we have to play and do other things we want to do. What we do in our work allows us to provide value to others and providing value to others contributes to our own self-esteem. Continuing to earn a living can finance our play and other non-work activities.

Working past normal retirement age, even part-time, can dramatically change how much we need to have in our retirement savings accounts, reducing financial pressure and providing dollars that can be spent and enjoyed now. In addition, it can provide a hedge against future inflation. Planning our work and making it fun will reduce the work stress we often feel in our lives.

So how do we analyze our work?

1. Am I working because I want to, or because I have to?
2. Do I enjoy what I do?
3. If I do enjoy my work, how much longer do I see myself doing it?
4. If I don't enjoy my work, are there things I could change to make work better?
5. Is there another type of work I would rather be doing?
6. And if I really enjoy my work, do I really want to put a time limit on how long I work or do I just want to control how work fits in with my other priorities?

Liking what you do and feeling that it provides value—that others appreciate—seems to be a key.

Many of our clients like what they're doing and really don't see themselves stopping any time soon. However, they might want to restructure their job to work fewer hours, or to focus on doing certain things and delegating the rest to others. This leaves more time to do the personal things they want to do.

Some clients aren't happy with their work situation, but recognize that if they could get rid of some of the aggravation and only do the things they like to do, they would consider continuing to work for a few more years.

Then there are those clients who are so fed-up with their job that they can't wait to get out. While I can empathize with them, I counsel them not to be too hasty because when they finish their first pass at the four steps, they might discover that they don't have the financial wherewithal to achieve their vision for the future. Working a few more years could make all the difference.

The process might take a few iterations in order to position things just the way they want them to be, but it is worth the effort if they end up with the life they want. After all, we're living longer. Don't we want to enjoy those added years?

Consider a teacher who is tired of classroom work. Having completed the necessary years of teaching, it would be possible to retire, but the teacher really doesn't want to leave education. Wouldn't it be great for this teacher if he or she could make an arrangement whereby he or she could continue to contribute to education but in a different capacity?

As I mentioned earlier, my wife and I are committed to the notion of making education more interesting to children so they are more motivated to learn. We are working with an organization that is well-positioned to provide an environment that would encourage and assist educator entrepreneurs who have ideas to develop them, get funding, and bring them in to reality. The teachers themselves can now continue to bring value within the educational arena, long past their normal retirement point. They can continue to earn and supplement their nest egg, and also have more time to enjoy the things they like to do.

I'm very excited about the possibilities, and I'm working with this group to create the infrastructure that will nurture these projects and bring them to the classrooms.

The decision whether to work full-time, part-time, or no longer will be different for everyone. Having other financial resources in the form of savings, a pension, or a spouse working, can change the financial perspective enormously and provide lots of flexibility.

Remember . . . the happier you are at work, the longer you may be able to work. The longer you work, the less often you'll have to dip into your investments. The longer you can avoid dipping into your investments, the more financially secure your future can be.

Some people are starting to wake up to the New Retirement Paradigm™ on their own. My swim coach Bruce decided to follow his passion. He quit his job as an engineer and became a full-time swim coach. He now has a 2012 US Olympic team qualifier to his credit along with a number of students who have received college swimming scholarships. The dream continues as he is planning to build his own aquatic center. Bruce has realized that many swim coaches don't think about retirement. They improve their coaching skills as they build athletes and many are still coaching well into their 70s and 80s. And the financial compensation often gets better each and every year as well.

Mike's Story

Another client, Mike, a podiatrist, was feeling the stress of having several practices. He was ready to throw in the towel, but admitted that there were some aspects of what he did that he really enjoyed.

It took a couple of years, but he was able to sell the parts of his practice that he didn't enjoy so much and focus more on the parts he liked. He and his wife downsized their home and he began taking more time off. In that time, they purchased a cottage in Massachusetts that he is renovating. He also found time to participate in a triathlon.

That one triathlon led to others and he found the time to train for and complete an Iron Man competition, a 2.4-mile swim followed by a 112-mile bike race followed by a full marathon. Fourteen hours later Mike was "an Iron Man."

He and his wife are eagerly anticipating a trip to Italy this year and spending more time at their cottage.

Define Your Personal (non-work) Life

- Where do you want to spend more time?
- Consider the ridiculous, maybe it can happen.
- What is the time/dollar balance you need to have?

CHAPTER 6

Define Your Vision of your Play Life

The next step in the process is to define how you want to spend your personal life. Too often, when asked, our clients tell us they want to spend more time with their grandchildren, or they want to travel. Some say they want to play more golf. But these goals are vague and unspecific.

I live in an over-55 community filled with residents who wanted to spend more time with their grandchildren. One day they woke up and realized they had become the day-care providers and couldn't do the other things they wanted to do. They were still living their lives around the school schedule they thought they were done with years before!

Because they didn't plan other things, they ended up babysitting five days a week and now don't have time to do those other things.

Our clients who are approaching retirement often talk about wanting to travel. But when we ask them where they want to go, they really don't know. And sometimes they procrastinate on traveling because they're afraid they'll deplete their nest egg and find themselves in financial trouble later.

I've learned that in order to achieve success, goals should be specific and measurable. Just think of goals as dreams with deadlines. If you want to spend more time with grandchildren ask yourself, "How much time?" Then develop plans for what you would like to do on the days you're not seeing your grandkids.

Clients Ken and Ruth became involved with an international organization, Questers. The mission of the group is to stimulate an appreciation of antiques and collecting them; and to encourage the preservation and restoration of existing historical landmarks. They enjoy the search and the joy that comes from finding. Ken and Ruth have gotten so involved that they've been officers at the state level and have even participated in planning annual conventions. They golf, help with caring for grandchildren, and are active in their retirement community.

Another client, a pathologist, has been a passionate student of butterflies for many years. He actually discovered a new species of butterfly while exploring the Pine Barrens of New Jersey. Reaching a point where his job was becoming more and more stressful, he negotiated a schedule that now allows him to work three weeks on and two weeks off. He and his wife are using this time to travel and think about what they want their lives to be like moving forward. He will probably always work in some capacity, but work will be redefined.

If travel is on your bucket list, decide where you want to go. Not sure? Visit a travel agent or subscribe to some good travel magazines. Start traveling on the Internet. Public television has numerous travel shows. National Geographic has lots of educational trips. Once you have a list of a few places you want to see, choose one and start making the arrangements.

Have a hobby? Carve out time to pursue it further. Want a hobby? Start testing the waters. Go to hobby stores; seek out groups that are of the same mind-set as you, sign up for a class, take advantage of the Internet and do some research. All of these ideas are ways to find something you enjoy and that relaxes you.

Community involvement might be on your list of things you would like to be more involved in. Volunteering can be extremely satisfying, and in today's tight economy, volunteers can make the difference in keeping important programs alive.

One of our clients decided to create an informal family foundation that helps local individuals and families who need a helping hand. In addition to aiding people in need, this has been an opportunity to impart family values about caring about others to their children and grandchildren.

Everyone is invited to bring a need to the attention of the family and the family decides how to help. The family foundation has paid for school lunches for a needy family, outfitted some school children with backpacks loaded with the school supplies, collected and shipped sports equipment to military units overseas who then give them out to the local children in efforts to improve relations with the local inhabitants, and they've even given money for a suitable work wardrobe to a young college student who got an internship at a network news organization. The grandchildren are learning to be aware of those less fortunate and they're also learning the joy of giving.

In our younger years we're often busy working and raising children, which pretty much absorbs our time. As we transition from those years to years with fewer responsibilities, we have a fantastic opportunity to expand our interests—if we take the time to think and plan it out. Work might continue to play a role, but in a different way.

Of course, all these activities require good health. A young client of mine decided that he needed to drop some weight and improve his health. He decided to start running, and as a goal, he wanted to run the Disney World Marathon. When he arrived at the venue, he learned that by earning a medal he could enjoy the park, free of charge.

After the race was over and he proudly entered the park with his medal, he noticed some people walking around with two medals. It turns out that by running the half-marathon and the full marathon, they won the "Goofy Medal."

One year later, Bryan got "goofy." He earned his Goofy Medal. His health is improved and he is working on his next set of goals.

Judy's Story

Our client Judy was burned out working in her 9-5 job. As she was entering her sixties, she felt that she had enough of working and wanted to retire. But from a financial standpoint, this wouldn't have given her the life she wanted to have. A little investigation revealed that one of the clients she serviced was willing to hire her on a consulting basis for about six months of the year. This would leave her free to enjoy the other six months doing what she wanted to do. The income from the consulting job, coupled with some pensions from previous employers, was enough to support her.

After two or three years, Judy was not sure she wanted to continue the consulting arrangement. She was struggling with that decision as well as when to begin collecting Social Security. At our regular meeting where she shared her concerns, she commented, "But I realize that I'm a renewable resource." This really captured the concept in a nutshell. Judy could decide from one year to the next whether to continue. She was providing value to the client, and as long as she did, she would be in the driver's seat. Every year Judy continues to work she is making her future years more secure.

Build the Financial Infrastructure to Support Your New Life

- Strategically layer your goals.
- Understand the role that work can continue to play.
- Understand the role that your investments need to play and how they strategically need to be positioned.

CHAPTER 7

Build the Financial Infrastructure to Support Your New Life

Now that you have an idea of how you want to spend your next few decades, it's time to take a step back and review your financial life. Is it healthy enough to support what you hope to do?

When we work with our clients, we guide them through a process of prioritizing their "needs" vs. their "wants" vs. their "wishes." Because some won't be able to do everything they want, we begin by making sure their basic, must-have "needs" are being met by their plan. By having this foundation in place they shouldn't have to be financially dependent on anyone.

The next category of goals is the "wants," or the things that make life more enjoyable. These could be dinners out, entertaining, travel, buying a new car periodically, gifts to family and friends, and charitable contributions, to name a few. This is an area where prioritizing can help with a financial infrastructure that can support a lifestyle.

And finally there are the "wishes." Wishes are those goals that are sort of pie-in-the-sky. These could be leaving a specific dollar amount to their children, creating a charitable foundation, memorializing themselves at an alma mater, and so on. Not everyone will be in a position to do something like this, but it doesn't hurt to dream. There might be a way to create a lasting legacy that doesn't involve hundreds and thousands of dollars.

Once the goals are prioritized and if it is determined that the financial plan won't support them completely, the client has several options. He or she can scale back his or her goals, or look for ways to increase financial resources.

Recently, a married couple discovered in their planning process that the second home they owned at the beach was much more costly than they had previously realized. They had the choice of keeping the summer home, versus enjoying the travel they envisioned. They decided to keep the home for a couple more years and then sell it when the husband fully retires so they can increase the time they spend traveling.

Continuing to work is a great solution, if circumstances permit. It doesn't have to be full-time; it doesn't even have to be in the same capacity as in the past. Whatever the work environment, if the client doesn't have to dip into savings to support a lifestyle for a few years, it can make a huge difference.

In any case, it is important to monitor and marshal financial resources so that twenty years into retirement the funds don't run out.

This concept really hit home with me when I heard a story about a very successful businesswoman who retired in her mid-sixties. Her family history was filled with relatives who died by the time they were seventy, so she wanted to pack as much into her remaining years as possible. Embarking on a series of travel adventures, she invited family and friends to join her as her guest. It wasn't too many years before she had pretty much used up most of her resources. Imagine her dismay when she lived well beyond her expectations and had to scrimp to get by.

Unlike many who opt for cliff retirement, this woman did have a plan . . . unfortunately it wasn't a complete plan. She didn't analyze all the options and all the possibilities. She didn't allow for contingencies.

What we do for our clients is challenge them with the right questions to provoke the thought process, and we act as their "accountability coach" to help bring them to a happy ending.

The New Retirement Paradigm™ is here.

Many of our clients are rethinking and changing their lives. They are excited about the present and the future.

You too can join the ranks of the luckiest people in the world. It's a journey well worth taking and worth the effort.

ABOUT THE AUTHOR

Ray Loewe's mission is to meet with clients and to get them feeling better about their financial future. His Unique Ability™ enables him to sift through the clutter of his clients' financial concerns and help find the best solutions, often using and sharing new perspectives in the process. This ability led to the development of The College Money System™, The New Retirement Paradigm™, and Wealth & Wisdom Sharing™ as ways of helping clients define their concerns and visualize their opportunities.

He has appeared on *Good Morning America*, CNNfn, and CNBC. He has been frequently quoted in national and local newspapers and magazines, including the *Wall Street Journal* and *Money Magazine*. Professional organizations often feature Ray as a speaker, including the Maryland Bar Association, the Annual Forum of The Society of Financial Service Professionals, and local Estate Planning Council and FPA groups.

Ray has authored four books, including his most recent book, *How to Plan for College: An Advisor's Guide to Acquiring New Clients and Profitable Assets*, which was released by The National Underwriting Company in 2007.

Ray is a Registered Representative and Investment Advisory Representative with United Planners Financial Services of America, Member FINRA and SIPC.

Ray holds a BS in Electrical Engineering from the University of Pennsylvania and an MBA from the Wharton School, University of Pennsylvania, and is a Chartered Life Underwriter (CLU) and a Chartered Financial Consultant (ChFC).

rloewe@financialresourcesnetwork.com
www.financialresourcesnetwork.com

CPSIA information can be obtained at www.ICGtesting.com
Printed in the USA
LVOW11s0016180614

390407LV00001B/10/P